Arizona Driver's Workbook

320+ Practice Driving Questions to Help You Pass the Arizona Learner's Permit Test

Connect Prep

Copyright © 2021 by Connect Prep

ALL RIGHTS RESERVED
No part of this book may be reproduced, stored in a retrieval system, or transmitted in any form or by any means, electronic, mechanical, photocopying, recording, scanning, or otherwise, without the prior written permission of the publisher.

Foreword:

In order to obtain your learner's permit, you must score at least an 85% on your permit test.

This book will prepare you for the knowledge that you will need to earn a passing grade on your learner's permit exam.

The Department of Motor Vehicles in your state issues official driving manuals which contain valuable resources that you must be familiar with and be knowledgeable on. If that information over-rides anything in this manual, be sure to memorize it and use it.

To achieve success with this book, use this as a fundamental tool to help guide you and better prepare you for the questions you will need to answer to pass your exam. The driving exam features a variety of questions that will gauge your quick-thinking skills and require you to use common sense. The questions featured in this book will help you to understand what to expect come test-time and will help better your chances for earning your learner's permit.

How to Use:

This book is best used when starting at the beginning working through to the end and taking time and thinking through each scenario. Applying your comprehension skills to best assess each question in detail will allow you to gain a better understanding and prepare you for your learner's permit exam. Imagining each scenario will help you to recall that image on the test itself.

You can choose to practice with an adult or a partner or read the questions aloud to yourself to retain them more easily. Practice is key, and this book is closely modeled after the chapters from the DMV manual.

Another good study technique is to use an index card to cover the answer choices, then read the scenario and question. Stop and think to yourself what the answer should be, then look for it in the choices. Most of the time it will be there because you studied the correct information, and you can move on. If not immediately identified, go back to the question being asked and eliminate answers until you get one that seems correct. Practicing like this will help you during the test because you won't get distracted by all of the choices and allow you to move quickly through any timed test.

By studying this book, you will be prepared and ready, and are likely to have better success when it comes to passing your exam. On average, nearly 50% of teenagers fail the exam on their first attempt. Allow this book to be the guide you need to earn a passing grade the first time.

Disclaimer: Due to laws changing frequently across states, please refer to your official local DMV manual for the most up-to-date answers and explanations.

ROAD SIGNS
Questions & Answers

1) What does this sign mean?

A. A tourist information center is ahead, stop if needed
B. A T-intersection is ahead; yield to cross traffic
C. A side road is ahead; watch for vehicles entering the roadway
D. A four-way intersection is ahead; prepare to yield

Correct Answer is B. A T-intersection is ahead; yield to cross traffic.

2) What does this road sign mean?

A. Prepare to stop
B. It indicates the direction the traffic flows
C. Go straight
D. There is a rest area open to the right

Correct Answer is B. It indicates the direction the traffic flows.

3) What does this sign indicate?

A. Traffic is merging ahead
B. A divided highway starts ahead
C. One-way traffic is ahead
D. The divided highway ends ahead

Correct Answer is D. A divided highway ends ahead.

4) What does this sign mean?

A. A yield sign ahead
B. A Y-intersection ahead
C. A youth hostel ahead
D. A side road ahead

Correct Answer is B. A Y-intersection ahead.

5) What do these double arrows mean?

A. Divided highway begins
B. Traffic may flow on both sides
C. Divided highway ends
D. Two-way traffic is ahead

Correct Answer is B. Traffic may flow on both sides.

6) What does this sign indicate?

A. Speed advisory on ramp
B. Speed limit ahead
C. Speed advisory at exit
D. Speed advisory at roundabout

Correct Answer is D. Speed advisory at roundabout.

7) **If you see this sign and you are traveling slower than most traffic, you should**

A. Move into the left lane
B. Take the next exit
C. Move into right lane
D. Increase your speed

Correct Answer is C. Move into right lane.

8) **When you see this road sign, you should**

A. Exit the highway with a minimum speed of 30 mph
B. Increase your speed to 30 mph and pass the vehicle in front of you
C. Exit the highway with a maximum speed of 60 mph
D. Exit the highway with a speed of 30 mph or less

Correct Answer is D. Exit the highway with a speed of 30 mph or less.

9) What does this traffic sign mean?

A. Turning right is prohibited after 1,000 feet
B. There is construction ahead in 1,000 feet
C. A parking zone is ahead
D. An alternate route is 1,000 feet ahead

Correct Answer is D. An alternate route is 1,000 feet ahead.

10) This sign represents

A. The number of miles to the next exit
B. The speed limit on the interstate
C. The exit number
D. The interstate highway number

Correct Answer is D. The interstate highway number.

11) This sign indicates that

A. Parking is allowed only for people with disabilities
B. U-turns are not allowed
C. Parking is not allowed
D. The road ahead is closed permanently

Correct Answer is C. Parking is not allowed.

12) This sign indicates that

A. A median is ahead
B. The road ahead has a dip
C. The road ahead has a bump
D. A hill grade is ahead

Correct Answer is C. The road ahead has a bump.

13) What does this sign indicate?

A. No right turn
B. Sharp right turn
C. Traffic merging from the right
D. Curve to the right

Correct Answer is B. Sharp right turn.

14) On this sign, the arrow means that

A. All vehicles must stop to make a right turn
B. The lane ahead is reserved for trucks to turn right
C. Drivers may choose in which direction they can go
D. All traffic must go only in the direction for the arrow

Correct Answer is D. All traffic must go only in the direction for the arrow.

15) If you see this sign, it means you are

A. Driving the wrong way
B. In a city
C. In the wrong lane
D. On an expressway

Correct Answer is A. Driving the wrong way.

16) What does this sign mean?

A. You must change lanes
B. You must stop
C. You must go straight
D. You must turn left

Correct Answer is C. You must go straight.

17) What does this sign indicate?

A. Traffic in the right lane must go straight, and traffic in the second lane must turn right
B. Traffic in the right lane must merge right, and traffic in the second lane should go straight or merge right
C. Traffic in the right lane must turn right, and traffic in the second lane should go straight or turn right
D. Traffic in the right lane must turn right, and traffic in the second lane should go straight or turn left

Correct Answer is C. Traffic in the right lane must turn right, and traffic in the second lane should go straight or turn right.

18) This sign indicates that

A. Vehicles on the left must turn left and vehicles on the right must merge with the right lane
B. Vehicles on the left must turn left and vehicles on the right may go straight or turn right
C. Vehicles on the left must turn left and vehicles on the right must turn right
D. Vehicles on the left must turn left and vehicles on the right must go straight

Correct Answer is B. Vehicles on the left must turn left and vehicles on the right may go straight or turn right.

19) What does this sign mean?

A. Traffic must make a right turn only
B. Traffic must make a left turn only
C. Traffic must merge left
D. Traffic must merge right

Correct Answer is B. Traffic must make a left turn only.

20) This sign warns the driver that the road is a

A. Winding road
B. Slippery road
C. Two-way road
D. Double curve

Correct Answer is A. Winding road.

KNOWLEDGE
Questions & Answers

1. What is the background color for work area signs?

    A. Yellow
    B. Orange
    C. Red
    D. White

Correct Answer is B. Orange.

2. What is the background color for warning signs?

    A. Yellow
    B. Orange
    C. Red
    D. White

Correct Answer is A. Yellow.

3. In the center of the two-lane road you are driving on, there is a solid line with a broken line beside it. You are on the side with the broken line. What does this mean?

    A. No passing is allowed
    B. Passing is permitted in either lane
    C. Passing is permitted for cars in your lane
    D. Passing is permitted for cars in the other lane

Correct Answer is C. Passing is permitted for cars in your lane.

4. You're stopped at a red light when a pedestrian steps into the crosswalk in front of you. The light turns green while the pedestrian is in front of your car. What should you do?

    A. Let the pedestrian cross the entire road before you go
    B. Honk the horn to let the pedestrian know they have made a mistake
    C. Inch forward so that the pedestrian knows to get out of the way of vehicles
    D. Wait for the pedestrian to clear the width of your vehicle before you go

Correct Answer is A. Let the pedestrian cross the entire road before you go.

5. You are driving on the highway when you notice a vehicle with emergency lights activated on the side of the road. What must you do?

    A. Move over into the next lane
    B. Slow down
    C. Both A and B
    D. Stop to see if you can help

Correct Answer is C. Both A and B.

6 You are driving on the highway when you notice a vehicle with yellow hazard lights activated on the side of the road. What must you do?

    A. Move over into the next lane
    B. Slow down
    C. Both A and B
    D. Stop to see if you can help

Correct Answer is A. Move over into the next lane.

7. What is the proper driver's hand signal for a right turn?

    A. Arm extended straight out the window to the left
    B. Arm extended straight out and bent up at the elbow to make a perpendicular angle
    C. Arm extended straight out and bent down at the elbow to make a perpendicular angle
    D. Pointing ahead to the roadway where you intend to turn

Correct Answer is B. Arm extended straight out and bent up at the elbow to make a perpendicular angle.

8. Now your brake lights are malfunctioning. What is the proper driver's hand signal to indicate that you plan to stop?

    A. Arm extended straight out the window to the left
    B. Arm extended straight out and bent up at the elbow to make a perpendicular angle
    C. Arm extended straight out and bent down at the elbow to make a perpendicular angle
    D. Pointing ahead to the roadway where you intend to turn

Correct Answer is C. Arm extended straight out and bent down at the elbow to make a perpendicular angle.

9. Which lane is ordinarily used for passing another vehicle?

    A. The left lane
    B. The right lane
    C. The shoulder
    D. Trick question! Passing is illegal

Correct Answer is A. The left lane.

10. There is a solid double yellow center line on your two-way roadway. What does this mean?

    A. You're on your own to determine whether to pass
    B. You may not pass
    C. Only trucks are permitted to pass
    D. You are near a hospital

Correct Answer is B. You may not pass.

11. You are in a two-way roadway with a broken yellow line, but up ahead you see that it turns into a solid double yellow line. You may not begin to pass a vehicle unless ...

    A. You have reached the solid double line
    B. You have not yet reached the solid double line
    C. You are able to finish passing before you reach the solid double line
    D. You wave to signal any oncoming vehicles

Correct Answer is C. You are able to finish passing before you reach the solid double line.

12. Never pass on the left on a two-way roadway if ...

    A. You are approaching a curve or top of a hill that you cannot see around or over
    B. You are within 100 feet of a railroad crossing
    C. You are within 100 feet of a bridge, tunnel or viaduct and your view is obstructed
    D. Any of the above

Correct Answer is D. Any of the above.

13. You are driving in the left lane of a road with two lanes traveling in the same direction, and you notice that a lot of cars are passing you on the right. What should you do?

    A. Slow down to make it easier for the cars to pass
    B. Go over the speed limit so that you are not the slowpoke
    C. Get out of the left lane, which is also known as the passing lane
    D. Maintain your speed; don't let yourself be pressured by other drivers

Correct Answer is C. Get out of the left lane, which is also known as the passing lane.

14. A school bus is approaching from the other direction. It stops and begins to flash its red lights. What must you do?

    A. Slow way down to keep children safe
    B. Move carefully past it
    C. Treat it like a stop sign; stop and go when it seems safe to do so
    D. Stop. You can proceed again when the red lights are no longer flashing

Correct Answer is D. Stop. You can proceed again when the red lights are no longer flashing.

15. You see a bus that looks and is equipped exactly like a school bus, but the people inside aren't children. Its red lights are flashing. What should you do?

    A. Treat it like a school bus, including stopping and not driving past it until the lights stop flashing
    B. Treat it like a school bus, including slowing way down to go past it
    C. Treat it like a school bus, including stopping for a moment and then moving on
    D. Treat it like any other vehicle; it is not necessary to stop for non-school buses

Correct Answer is A. Treat it like a school bus, including stopping and not driving past it until the lights stop flashing.

16. You are parking on a downhill slope. What should you do?

    A. Put your car in "park" (or if you have a manual transmission, first gear)
    B. Turn your wheels toward the curb
    C. Put on your parking brake
    D. All of the above

Correct Answer is D. All of the above.

17. What should you do when you encounter a "yield" sign where two lanes come together?

    A. Treat it like a stop sign and stop
    B. Trust that a car approaching from another lane will pause to let you go
    C. Allow all cars from the other lane go before entering the roadway
    D. Take turns entering the roadway with cars in the other lane

Correct Answer is C. Allow all cars from the other lane go before entering the roadway.

18. What color and shape are a yield sign?

    A. Red and white triangle
    B. Yellow and black triangle
    C. Red and white octagon
    D. Yellow and black circle

Correct Answer is A. Red and white triangle.

19. You spot a speed limit sign ahead, and it will take you from a 35 mph zone to a 25 mph zone. What does the law say about when the speed limit is officially 25 mph?

    A. Exactly at the point where the sign is located
    B. 25 yards before the sign
    C. 25 yards after the sign
    D. Speed limits are always approximate

Correct Answer is A. Exactly at the point where the sign is located.

20. What is the term for "driving to save lives, time, and money, in spite of the conditions around you and the actions of others"?

    A. Assertive driving
    B. Protective driving
    C. Defensive driving
    D. Confident driving

Correct Answer is C. Defensive driving.

21. You're at a railroad crossing and the gate is down, but you can see the train, and it is moving at an extremely low rate of speed. When is it OK to go around the gate?

    A. Never
    B. After sounding your car's horn at the engineer
    C. After hearing the train's "go ahead" whistle
    D. Whenever your best judgment says you can go

Correct Answer is A. Never.

22. When you must stop at a railroad crossing, what is the minimum distance your car can be from the tracks?

    A. 5 feet
    B. 10 feet
    C. 15 feet
    D. 20 feet

Correct Answer is C. 15 feet.

23. What must you do from one-half hour after the sun sets until one-half hour before it rises?

    A. Take a driving break
    B. Turn on your headlights
    C. Check your tire pressure
    D. Wear sunglasses

Correct Answer is B. Turn on your headlights.

24. What rights do bicyclists have to the road?

    A. They have the right to share the road and travel in the same direction as motor vehicles
    B. They have the right to share the road but must face traffic
    C. They belong on sidewalks
    D. They can be on the road, but they must yield to drivers

Correct Answer is A. They have the right to share the road and travel in the same direction as motor vehicles.

25. What rights do in-line skaters have to the road?

    A. They have the right to share the road and travel in the same direction as motor vehicles
    B. They have the right to share the road but must face traffic
    C. They belong on sidewalks
    D. They can be on the road but they must yield to drivers

Correct Answer is A. They have the right to share the road and travel in the same direction as motor vehicles.

26. What responsibilities do bicyclists have?

    A. They must obey all traffic signs and signals
    B. They must use hand signals when turning, slowing/stopping, and changing lanes
    C. They must keep at least one hand on the handlebars at all times
    D. All of the above

Correct Answer is D. All of the above.

27. A slow-moving vehicle symbol must be displayed on the back of vehicles drawn by animals, most farm vehicles and some construction equipment. What color is the reflective sign?

    A. Yellow
    B. Orange
    C. White
    D. Blue

Correct Answer is B. Orange.

28. What does a yellow curb mean?

    A. You may park there for an hour
    B. No parking allowed
    C. You may only stop enough to load or unload
    D. None of the above

Correct Answer is C. You may only stop enough to load or unload.

29. May a vehicle leave the paved portion of the roadway to pass another vehicle on the right?

   A. No
   B. Yes, any time
   C. Yes, when passing a vehicle that is turning left
   D. Yes, for purposes of parking

Correct Answer is A. No.

30. A roundabout is a feature where multiple roads enter into a route that circles a central island. When you enter a roundabout, what should you never do?

   A. Look to your left
   B. Enter when there is a pause in traffic
   C. Make a left turn
   D. Slow down before entering

Correct Answer is C. Make a left turn.

31. Who has the right of way when you enter a roundabout?

    A. You
    B. Vehicles already within the roundabout
    C. Vehicles displaying their turn signals
    D. The vehicle at the next entrance to the right

Correct Answer is B. Vehicles already within the roundabout.

32. What steps should you take when exiting a roundabout?

    A. Drive slowly
    B. Use your right turn signal
    C. Both A and B
    D. Accelerate

Correct Answer is B. Use your right turn signal.

33. In a roundabout, three of these actions are forbidden, but one is allowed. Which one is permitted?

    A. Stopping except to avoid a crash
    B. Taking more than one revolution around the center island
    C. Changing lanes
    D. Passing large trucks

Correct Answer is B. Taking more than one revolution around the center island.

34. Vehicles that are part of a funeral procession must do which of the following?

    A. Turn on their flashing emergency lights
    B. Display a flag or decal from the funeral home
    C. Keep all windows up
    D. Give other drivers the right of way

Correct Answer is B. Display a flag or decal from the funeral home.

35. **For those vehicles that are not involved in a funeral procession, which of these rules apply?**

    A. Take special care when driving between vehicles that are part of the moving procession
    B. Merge into the procession to obtain right of way
    C. Do not attempt to pass any vehicle in the procession
    D. Turn on your own flashing emergency lights

Correct Answer is C. Do not attempt to pass any vehicle in the procession.

36. **Which of the following is the term used to describe an uncontrolled display of anger by the driver of a vehicle (usually in response to actions by another driver)?**

    A. Road rage
    B. Angry operation
    C. Driver aggression
    D. Road war

Correct Answer is A. Road rage.

37. In which of these areas should you park?

    A. In an intersection
    B. On a bridge
    C. In a marked parking space
    D. Blocking a fire hydrant

Correct Answer is C. In a marked parking space.

38. When you are on a road that has three or more lanes traveling in the same direction and none of them are specially marked, what is the purpose of the lane farthest to the left?

    A. To accommodate large trucks
    B. To be used only by emergency vehicles
    C. To allow carpoolers to move freely
    D. To allow vehicles to pass other, slower vehicles

Correct Answer is D. To allow vehicles to pass other, slower vehicles.

39. When you are about to turn a corner, which technique should you use?

    A. The hand-over-hand technique
    B. Hands at 10 o'clock and 2 o'clock
    C. The one-hand-only technique
    D. The method that feels most comfortable

Correct Answer is A. The hand-over-hand technique.

40. You hear a siren or see flashing red or blue lights behind you on the road. What must you do?

    A. Pull over to the left side of the road
    B. Speed up
    C. Pull over to the right side of the road
    D. Stop in the middle of the road

Correct Answer is C. Pull over to the right side of the road.

41. A sign shows a white capital H on a blue background. What does it mean?

    A. Help available
    B. Hospital
    C. High-efficiency vehicles only
    D. Hotel

Correct Answer is B. Hospital.

42. A school bus in the opposite lane has stopped to pick up or drop of student passengers. In which instance do you not have to stop?

    A. You are on a divided highway
    B. You are moving in the opposite direction of the bus
    C. The bus does not display a stop sign
    D. No students are visible

Correct Answer is A. You are on a divided highway.

43. You see a white sign showing a black delivery-type truck with a red backslash/prohibition symbol over it. What does this mean?

    A. Trucks are not permitted on this road
    B. Pickup trucks are not permitted on this road
    C. Deliveries are not allowed on this road
    D. Black trucks are prohibited

Correct Answer is A. Trucks are not permitted on this road.

44. You're going the wrong way. Is it OK to make a U-turn?

    A. Always, if there is no oncoming traffic
    B. Always, if you have 100 yards of visibility
    C. Never; U-turns are illegal
    D. Sometimes, depending on state and local laws

Correct Answer is D. Sometimes, depending on state and local laws.

45. Pedestrians have the right-of-way over vehicles in these instances:

    A. When they are in a marked crosswalk
    B. When they are in an intersection
    C. Both A and B
    D. Always

Correct Answer is C. Both A and B.

46. There is a bicycle in your lane of a two-lane road, and you want to pass it; however, another vehicle is approaching in the opposite lane. What do you do?

    A. Speed up to get around the bike before the car can reach you
    B. Honk your horn at the biker to let them know you're passing
    C. Wait for the other vehicle to go by before you pass the bike
    D. Cautiously pass between the bike and the vehicle

Correct Answer is C. Wait for the other vehicle to go by before you pass the bike.

47. When stopping at a railroad crossing, how much space should you leave between your vehicle and the tracks?

    A. 15 to 50 feet
    B. 10 to 20 feet
    C. 5 feet
    D. 30 feet

Correct Answer is A. 15 to 50 feet.

48. The minimum speed on an interstate highway under normal conditions is ...

    A. 65 mph
    B. 50 mph
    C. 40 mph
    D. 25 mph

Correct Answer is C. 40 mph.

49. You see a yellow sign featuring three arrows forming a circle. What does this mean?

    A. You are approaching a roundabout
    B. You must turn around
    C. There is a detour ahead
    D. You are approaching a school drop-off zone

Correct Answer is A. You are approaching a roundabout.

50. What is the purpose of an acceleration lane?

    A. To let you pass a car on the left on a divided highway
    B. To let you increase your speed to that of traffic you're merging with on a highway
    C. To slow down so that other cars can pass you
    D. To pull off a highway

Correct Answer is B. To let you increase your speed to that of traffic you're merging with on a highway.

51. A sign shows a winding black arrow on a yellow background. What does it mean?

    A. The road ahead is curved
    B. Snakes have been seen on roadway
    C. Test your brakes before proceeding
    D. The road ahead is hilly

Correct Answer is A. The road ahead is curved.

52. What is true about a winding road sign?

    A. The road ahead has three or more curves
    B. Drivers should slow down
    C. There are potential hazards ahead
    D. All of the above

Correct Answer is D. All of the above.

53. What is true about a DO NOT ENTER sign?

    A. It is red and white
    B. There is a risk of collision beyond it
    C. It is usually found at the start of a road or on an exit ramp or crossover
    D. All of the above

Correct Answer is D. All of the above.

54. A sign shows a figure striding between two lines. What does this mean?

    A. Sidewalk in neighborhood
    B. Pedestrian crossing
    C. Crossing guard ahead
    D. Shopping district

Correct Answer is B. Pedestrian crossing.

55. During precipitation, you should double the space between you and the car in front of you. How many seconds apart should you be when it's raining out?

    A. 2 seconds
    B. 4 seconds
    C. 6 seconds
    D. 8 seconds

Correct Answer is D. 8 seconds.

56. A yellow road sign depicts an X with two R's on it. What does this mean?

    A. Road work
    B. Roundabout
    C. Right of way
    D. Railroad

Correct Answer is D. Railroad.

57. What color of line typically marks the left edge of the pavement on a four-lane divided road?

    A. Yellow
    B. White
    C. Black
    D. Red

Correct Answer is A. Yellow.

58. What color of line typically marks the right edge of the pavement on a four-lane divided road?

    A. Yellow
    B. White
    C. Black
    D. Red

Correct Answer is B. White.

59. What should you not do as you drive through a work zone?

   A. Move over
   B. Speed up
   C. Read signs
   D. Watch out for workers

Correct Answer is B. Speed up.

60. What should you be sure to do when you pass a car on the left on a two-lane road?

   A. Signal when entering and exiting left lane
   B. Wave at the other driver
   C. Increase speed by 20 mph
   D. Flash your headlights at the car you are passing

Correct Answer is A. Signal when entering and exiting left lane.

61. You miss your exit on a limited-access highway. What should you do?

   A. Move to the shoulder and back up to the exit
   B. U-turn and backtrack to your exit
   C. Drive to the next exit and drive back to the exit that way
   D. Drive off road to the exit

Correct Answer is C. Drive to the next exit and drive back to the exit that way.

62. What should you not do when driving by an accident scene?

   A. Watch the road closely
   B. Slow down
   C. Examine the scene
   D. Watch for debris

Correct Answer is C. Examine the scene.

63. You see a yellow sign depicting a red octagon and a black arrow pointing straight ahead. What does this indicate?

    A. There is a traffic light ahead
    B. There is a stop sign ahead
    C. There is a railroad crossing ahead
    D. There is a dead end ahead

Correct Answer is B. There is a stop sign ahead.

64. How fast should you be going when you exit an on-ramp onto an expressway?

    A. Faster than traffic on the expressway
    B. Slower than the traffic on the expressway
    C. About the speed of traffic on the expressway
    D. 55 mph, no matter the speed of others

Correct Answer is C. About the speed of traffic on the expressway.

65. An electronic panel has a set of flashing arrows pointing in one direction. What does it mean?

    A. Move in the direction the arrows indicate
    B. Lane closes ahead
    C. Both A and B
    D. Neither A nor B

Correct Answer is C. Both A and B.

66. On wet roads, you should slow down to avoid this dangerous result.

    A. Flat tire
    B. Hydroplaning
    C. Drowsiness
    D. Stalling

Correct Answer is B. Hydroplaning.

67. Where does a solid yellow line appear on a one-way road?

    A. Right edge
    B. Left edge
    C. Center
    D. Across an intersection

Correct Answer is B. Left edge.

68. What does a red arrow mean?

    A. You must slow down when moving in the direction it indicates
    B. You must stop and then proceed with caution in the direction it indicates
    C. You may not move in the direction it indicates
    D. You should be prepared to stop frequently on the road ahead

Correct Answer is C. You may not move in the direction it indicates.

69. A white sign has black letters that spell out "FINES DOUBLE." Where would you see a sign like this?

    A. Near a construction zone
    B. In a no-parking zone
    C. At the start of a closed road
    D. At a state line

Correct Answer is A. Near a construction zone.

70. A narrow vertical sign has black and yellow diagonal stripes. What does this indicate?

    A. Object on or near the roadway
    B. Rumble strips ahead
    C. Do not enter
    D. School zone

Correct Answer is A. Object on or near the roadway.

71. On a roadway with three lanes of traffic moving in the same direction, where should slow traffic drive?

    A. In the far-left lane
    B. In the far-right lane
    C. In the center lane
    D. On the shoulder

Correct Answer is B. In the far-right lane.

72. When must a driver operate a turn signal?

    A. When changing lanes
    B. When preparing to turn
    C. When entering or pulling out of a parking space
    D. All of the above

Correct Answer is D. All of the above.

73. You meet another vehicle on a one-lane road hill where neither can pass. Which vehicle needs to back up so the other can pass?

    A. The one going downhill
    B. The one going uphill
    C. The larger vehicle
    D. The first one to give in

Correct Answer is B. The one going uphill.

74. What is an interchange?

    A. A parking area
    B. A junction of two or more highways to allow passage without crossing traffic streams
    C. Addresses exchanged in the event of an accident
    D. Money offered at a staffed tollbooth on a toll road

Correct Answer is B. A junction of two or more highways to allow passage without crossing traffic streams.

75. Which of these are not child safety rules that are the same in every state?

    A. Children may not travel in the arms of another passenger
    B. Children may never be left unattended in a vehicle
    C. Children may not eat or drink in a vehicle
    D. Smaller children must be restrained in federally approved car seats

Correct Answer is C. Children may not eat or drink in a vehicle.

76. A round sign has a white dash against a red background. What does this sign mean?

    A. Dead end ahead
    B. Bus does not stop here
    C. No parking
    D. Do not enter

Correct Answer is D. Do not enter.

77. The sign in front of you has a white background and shows a black arrow that goes straight up then bends at a right angle to the right. What does it mean?

   A. A sharp left turn is ahead
   B. A sharp right turn is ahead
   C. An intersection is ahead
   D. A rest area is off to the right ahead

Correct Answer is B. A sharp right turn is ahead.

78. A sign shows a straight arrow with a right arrow veering off from it. What does this signify?

   A. Avoid the right road and stay straight
   B. Avoid the straight road and stay right
   C. You have the choice of going straight or right
   D. Keep in the left lane

Correct Answer is C. You have the choice of going straight or right.

79. A yellow diamond-shaped sign lists dimensions (such as 12' 8") between arrows pointing both up and down. What do the dimensions indicate?

    A. Size of sign
    B. Average car dimensions
    C. Distance to rest area
    D. Height of a low-clearance overpass

Correct Answer is D. Height of a low-clearance overpass.

80. You arrive at an intersection with a flashing red signal. What does this mean?

    A. Road closed
    B. Proceed with caution
    C. Shift lanes
    D. Stop before proceeding

Correct Answer is D. Stop before proceeding.

81. A yellow diamond-shaped sign depicts a fire truck. What does this mean?

    A. There is a fire ahead
    B. Emergency vehicles may enter the roadway ahead
    C. School zone ahead
    D. Fire hydrant located ahead

Correct Answer is B. Emergency vehicles may enter the roadway ahead.

82. What's the rule about parking near a fire hydrant?

    A. Leave three feet of space for firefighter access
    B. Don't park within 15 feet in either direction
    C. Be prepared to move in case of fire
    D. Leave windows open for hose access in case of fire

Correct Answer is B. Don't park within 15 feet in either direction.

83. How far from a railroad crossing can you legally park?

    A. 10 feet
    B. 25 feet
    C. 50 feet
    D. 100 feet

Correct Answer is C. 50 feet.

84. How far must I park from a crosswalk at an intersection?

    A. 5 feet
    B. 10 feet
    C. 15 feet
    D. 20 feet

Correct Answer is D. 20 feet.

85. You arrive at a four-way intersection at the same time as another driver. Who goes first?

    A. The one who is waved on by the other driver
    B. The one in the larger vehicle
    C. The one on the left
    D. The one on the right

Correct Answer is D. The one on the right.

86. At an intersection, you like to be courteous and wave other vehicles on, whether or not they have the right of way. Is this a safe practice?

    A. Yes, because everyone knows what to do
    B. Yes, because nicer is better
    C. No, because traffic flow can be delayed
    D. No, because it is better just to be the one who goes

Correct Answer is C. No, because traffic flow can be delayed.

87. Who has the right of way at a T intersection?

    A. The driver on the road that intersects
    B. Drivers on the through road
    C. The driver who sounds the car's horn first
    D. The driver who is going the fastest

Correct Answer is B. Drivers on the through road.

88. The sign says, "NO PARKING ANY TIME." What is true about the no-parking zone?

    A. You may stop temporarily, but only for loading or unloading merchandise
    B. You may stop temporarily, but only to pick up a passenger
    C. Both A and B
    D. You must not stop for any reason

Correct Answer is C. Both A and B.

89. The traffic signal displays as a steady green light. What does this mean?

    A. Stop
    B. Proceed through the intersection
    C. Slow down and be prepared to stop
    D. Pause before proceeding

Correct Answer is B. Proceed through the intersection.

90. The traffic signal displays as a steady yellow light. What does this mean?

    A. Stop
    B. Proceed through the intersection
    C. Slow down and be prepared to stop
    D. Pause before proceeding

Correct Answer is C. Slow down and be prepared to stop.

91. The traffic signal displays as a steady red light. What does this mean?

    A. Stop
    B. Proceed through the intersection
    C. Slow down and be prepared to stop
    D. Pause before proceeding

Correct Answer is A. Stop.

92. The road sign says, "NO STANDING ANY TIME." What does this mean?

    A. You may stop temporarily, but only for loading or unloading merchandise
    B. You may stop temporarily, but only to pick up a passenger
    C. Both A and B
    D. You must not stop for any reason

Correct Answer is B. You may stop temporarily, but only to pick up a passenger.

93. A yellow diamond-shaped sign shows an arrow that rises straight briefly from the bottom, then bends slightly to the left, and then bends again back slightly to the right. What does this signify?

    A. Very windy road ahead
    B. Hilly road ahead
    C. Road ahead curves left, then right
    D. Road icy at times

Correct Answer is C. Road ahead curves left, then right.

94. Your high-beam headlights are on and a car is approaching in the opposite lane. You should dim your lights when the car is ___ feet away.

    A. 100
    B. 200
    C. 500
    D. 1,000

Correct Answer is C. 500.

95. Your high-beam headlights are on and you are following another vehicle. You should dim your lights when you are within ___ feet.

    A. 100
    B. 300
    C. 500
    D. 1,000

Correct Answer is B. 300.

96. What is required to park in a spot reserved for disabled persons?

    A. A disabled person parking permit
    B. An obvious disability
    C. A combination of A and B
    D. A disability that may be invisible

Correct Answer is A. A disabled person parking permit.

97. A yellow sign features the black outline of a moose. What is it trying to tell you?

    A. You might see a moose in a field — what a treat!
    B. You might encounter a moose crossing or standing in the road — proceed with caution
    C. There is a zoo ahead
    D. Tourist attraction ahead

Correct Answer is B. You might encounter a moose crossing or standing in the road — be careful.

98. Why should you not drive with low tire pressure?

    A. You could have a tire blowout
    B. You could lose control at high speeds
    C. You will experience lower fuel economy
    D. All of the above

Correct Answer is D. All of the above.

99. You are driving on an expressway when your oil pressure light — the one that looks like an oil can — comes on. What should you do?

    A. Drive calmly to the next intersection to get service
    B. Pull over and stop your car as soon as you can do so safely
    C. Add some oil to the car
    D. Make an appointment to get service when it's convenient

Correct Answer is B. Pull over and stop your car as soon as you can do so safely.

100. What does the law say about driving a passenger car with one headlight out?

    A. It's illegal — don't do it
    B. You will get a warning the first time you are pulled over
    C. You must use your bright headlights to compensate
    D. Use your hazard lights to compensate

Correct Answer is A. It's illegal — don't do it.

101. What should you do when approaching a yellow traffic light from half a block away?

A. Speed up to make it through the intersection
B. Slow down to cautiously make it through the intersection
C. Slow down to a stop; there's not enough time to make it through the intersection
D. Beep your horn as you proceed through the intersection

Correct Answer is C. Slow down to a stop; there's not enough time to make it through the intersection.

102. What's the safest way to deal with your phone while driving?

A. Use speaker, voice-to-text, and other hands-free settings
B. Use it as normal, but stop speaking or texting at intersections
C. Stow your phone away and check it when your trip is completed
D. Don't text — just talk

Correct Answer is C. Stow your phone away and check it when your trip is completed.

103. You're in the right lane of the two westbound lanes of a divided highway, and you're ready to pass the slower car in front of you. What do you do?

  A. Signal your intent to enter the left (passing) westbound lane, maintain your speed to pass the slower vehicle, and when you have sufficient room, signal to merge back into the right lane
  B. Stick to the left lane for the entirety of your drive so that you can avoid merging
  C. Stay where you are behind the slower car, just to be on the safe side
  D. Speed up by at least 20 mph to get around the slower car as quickly as you can

Correct Answer is A. Signal your intent to enter the left (passing) westbound lane, maintain your speed to pass the slower vehicle, and when you have sufficient room, signal to merge back into the right lane.

104. You are driving on an interstate when you see that you have a left-side exit coming up in two miles. What do you do?

  A. Move to the leftmost lane at your first safe opportunity so that you'll have plenty of time to get ready to exit
  B. Wait until the last opportunity to enter the leftmost lane so that you won't slow down faster traffic
  C. Stay in the right lane; interstates don't have left-side exits
  D. Straddle the line for the leftmost lane so that you'll be positioned to merge when the time comes

Correct Answer is A. Move to the leftmost lane at your first safe opportunity so that you'll have plenty of time to get ready to exit.

105. A car is stopped on the right shoulder of the highway. What should you do?

    A. Pull over and see if you can help
    B. Call 911
    C. Slow down and move to the left
    D. Maintain your speed and drive as normal

Correct Answer is C. Slow down and move to the left.

106. You are on a two-lane road with a solid double line in the middle. When is it OK to pass?

    A. You should never pass when there is a double-yellow line
    B. When you are at the top of a hill
    C. When you have cleared a curve
    D. When it appears safe to do so

Correct Answer is A. You should never pass when there is a double-yellow line.

107. Why does the state examiner check your vehicle before your driving test?

    A. To make sure it is safe to operate
    B. To look for cheat sheets
    C. To make sure it is sufficiently clean
    D. To make sure it is will be comfortable for the examiner

Correct Answer is A. To make sure it is safe to operate.

108. What's the best way to avoid a crash?

    A. Drive only in daylight
    B. Maintain appropriate distance
    C. Have airbags
    D. Keep your lights on

Correct Answer is B. Maintain appropriate distance.

109. How many drinks can affect your driving?

   A. One
   B. Two
   C. Three
   D. More than three

Correct Answer is A. One.

110. When is it OK to use a handicapped parking space?

   A. When you have a legally obtained handicapped hanging tag or license plate
   B. When you are hurt or sick
   C. When you are picking up a person with a handicapping condition
   D. All of the above

Correct Answer is A. When you have a legally obtained handicapped hanging tag or license plate.

111. What drugs can impede your ability to drive safely?

    A. Over-the-counter drugs
    B. Prescription drugs
    C. Alcohol
    D. All of the above

Correct Answer is D. All of the above.

112. You're entering a roundabout where traffic is already present. Who needs to yield?

    A. You
    B. The other vehicles
    C. Both
    D. Neither

Correct Answer is A. You.

113. The light is green, but traffic is backed up into the intersection. What should you do?

A. Proceed into the intersection with caution
B. Go around the traffic
C. Wait until you can fully clear the intersection before advancing
D. Beep your horn loudly as you enter the intersection

Correct Answer is C. Wait until you can fully clear the intersection before advancing.

114. How do you measure your following distance?

A. Consult mile marker signs
B. Calculate the time it takes for you to pass a fixed object after the car in front of you passes it
C. Use your odometer
D. Calculate the time it takes for the car behind you to pass a fixed object after you do

Correct Answer is B. Calculate the time it takes for you to pass a fixed object after the car in front of you passes it.

115. Why is it a bad idea to litter while driving?

    A. It's bad for the environment
    B. You can cause an accident
    C. You can be fined or go to jail for littering
    D. All of the above

Correct Answer is D. All of the above.

116. When should you put extra distance between you and the car in front of you?

    A. When the road is slick
    B. When you are going down a steep hill
    C. When you're following a motorcycle
    D. All of the above

Correct Answer is D. All of the above.

117. How many seconds should you maintain between your car and the next in ordinary conditions?

- A. Two
- B. Four
- C. Six
- D. Eight

Correct Answer is B. Four.

118. When parallel parking, your front and back wheels must be within how many inches of the curb?

- A. 5
- B. 12
- C. 18
- D. 20

Correct Answer is C. 18.

119. When you are ready to exit your parallel-parked vehicle, what should you be sure to check for?

    A. Passing vehicles
    B. Passing bicyclists
    C. Passing pedestrians
    D. All of the above

Correct Answer is D. All of the above.

120. Is it permissible to park in an electric vehicle charging space if you are not charging an electric vehicle?

    A. Yes
    B. No

Correct Answer is B. No.

121. You are turning left from a two-way street onto a one-way street. When you're done turning, what lane should you be in?

   A. Right lane
   B. Left lane
   C. Center lane
   D. Any lane

Correct Answer is B. Left lane.

122. How should you cross several freeway lanes?

   A. All at once
   B. One at a time
   C. You should not do this

Correct Answer is B. One at a time.

123. When should you not pass?

   A. Within 100 feet of an intersection
   B. Within 100 feet of a bridge, tunnel, or railroad crossing
   C. When you cannot see approaching traffic because of a hill or curve
   D. All of the above

Correct Answer is D. All of the above.

124. Is it OK to pass at an intersection?

   A. Yes
   B. No

Correct Answer is B. No.

125. When may you pass on the right?

A. When the driver ahead of you is turning left and you do not need to drive off the roadway to get around
B. When the shoulder is broad and paved
C. When a line of traffic is stopped for some reason and you want to get around
D. On a one-way street

Correct Answer is A. When the driver ahead of you is turning left and you do not need to drive off the roadway to get around.

126. When passing a bicyclist, how many feet should you allow between your vehicle and the bike?

A. 1
B. 3
C. 5
D. 7

Correct Answer is B. 3.

127. Why should you never drive in front of a large truck and suddenly stop?

    A. The truck may not be able to stop in time to avoid crashing into your vehicle
    B. Trucks always have the right of way
    C. Truck drivers may want to retaliate
    D. You should be especially courteous to truck drivers

Correct Answer is A. The truck may not be able to stop in time to avoid crashing into your vehicle.

128. Trucks have blind spots or "no-zones" where drivers may not be able to see you. These include the spaces directly behind the truck, directly beside the passenger-side front of the cab, or in the area beside either side of the trailer. To be sure you are not in a blind spot, make sure you can see ____.

    A. The logo on the side of the truck
    B. The emergency placards behind the truck
    C. The mud flaps of the truck
    D. The driver's reflection in the truck's side mirrors

Correct Answer is D. The driver's reflection in the truck's side mirrors.

129. How much distance do you need to keep when behind an active police car?

    A. 100 feet
    B. 200 feet
    C. 300 feet
    D. 500 feet

Correct Answer is C. 300 feet.

130. Which of the practices are dangerous with big trucks?

    A. Cutting them off to reach an exit or turn
    B. Lingering alongside them when passing
    C. Following too closely
    D. All of the above

Correct Answer is D. All of the above.

131. Which of the following may be classified as slow-moving vehicles?

   A. Farm equipment
   B. Animal-drawn carts
   C. Economy cars
   D. A & B

Correct Answer is D. A & B.

132. What kind of placard does a slow-moving vehicle display?

   A. Blue heart
   B. Yellow moon
   C. Green clover
   D. Orange triangle

Correct Answer is D. Orange triangle.

133. Is it legal to spook a horse that is drawing a vehicle?

A. Yes
B. Of course not

Correct Answer is B. Of course not.

134. How much of a following distance should you allow between your car and the motorcycle in front of you?

A. 2 seconds
B. 4 seconds
C. 8 seconds
D. 12 seconds

Correct Answer is B. 4 seconds.

135. What is a good way to avoid fatigue while driving?

A. Go faster to get to your destination before you fall asleep
B. Turn up the heat to maintain comfort
C. Drink an energy drink
D. Don't drive if you're feeling fatigued

Correct Answer is D. Don't drive if you're feeling fatigued.

136. Why should you maintain a steady speed and signal in advance before turning?

A. To maintain assured clear distance in front of your car
B. To maintain assured clear distance behind your car
C. To maintain appropriate distance beside your car
D. You should not do this

Correct Answer is B. To maintain assured clear distance behind your car.

137. What does a yellow sign indicate?

- A. Bathroom ahead
- B. Construction work ahead
- C. Hazard ahead
- D. Restaurants ahead

Correct Answer is C. Hazard ahead.

138. A yellow diamond-shaped sign indicates ___.

- A. Warning
- B. Available services
- C. Stop ahead
- D. Speed limit

Correct Answer is A. Warning.

139. What kind of signs have a white background?

    A. Regulatory
    B. Warning
    C. Route
    D. Service

Correct Answer is A. Regulatory.

140. At an intersection, you have a blinking red light, but the cross traffic has no signal. How do you proceed?

    A. Stop, let the first car from the cross-traffic pass, then take your turn
    B. Stop until there is a sufficient pause in cross-traffic to move
    C. Slow down as you move into the intersection
    D. Stop until it turns green

Correct Answer is B. Stop until there is a sufficient pause in cross-traffic to move.

141. You are in reverse and turning your steering wheel to the left. Which way will your car go?

A. Frontwards to the left
B. Frontwards to the right
C. Backwards to the left
D. Backwards to the right

Correct Answer is C. Backwards to the left.

142. How do the rights and responsibilities of bicyclists compare to those of car drivers?

A. Bicyclists have the same rights but fewer responsibilities
B. Bicyclists have fewer rights but the same responsibilities
C. Car drivers have all rights over bicyclists
D. Car drivers and bicyclists have the same rights and responsibilities

Correct Answer is D. Car drivers and bicyclists have the same rights and responsibilities.

143. Some responsibilities of bicyclists include the following:

    A. Obeying all traffic signs and signals
    B. Riding in the same direction as traffic
    C. Signaling when changing lanes or turning
    D. All of the above

Correct Answer is D. All of the above.

144. A bicyclist must yield to pedestrians.

    A. True
    B. False

Correct Answer is A. True.

145. A bicyclist must not ride on the sidewalk, unless the city specifically allows it.

   A. True
   B. False

Correct Answer is A. True

146. For a bicyclist operating in darkness, one of these is a best practice, while the others are laws. Can you pick out the item that is just a suggestion and not a law?

   A. Don't wear dark clothing
   B. Have a rear red reflector or light that is visible for 500 feet
   C. Have a white or yellow reflector on each pedal or the biker's shoes or ankles
   D. Have a reflector on the front or back wheel, or have reflectorized tires

Correct Answer is A. Don't wear dark clothing.

147. Bicyclists have the right to operate on city streets.

    A. True
    B. False

Correct Answer is A. True.

148. Bicyclists have the right to operate on freeways.

    A. True
    B. False
    C. True when not forbidden by a sign

Correct Answer is C. True when not forbidden by a sign.

149. How might you identify a pedestrian who is blind?

    A. Red-tipped white cane
    B. Presence of guide dog
    C. Sometimes you can't tell
    D. All of the above

Correct Answer is D. All of the above.

150. True or false: Pedestrians are always given the right of way:

    A. True
    B. False

Correct Answer is A. True.

151. What first steps should you take when you are being pulled over by an officer?

A. Turn on your right turn signal and slow down until you find the first opportunity to pull over
B. Speed up to meet the officer at the next exit
C. Wave out the window at the officer to acknowledge the officer's presence
D. Drive as normally until you find a good place to pull over

Correct Answer is A. Turn on your right turn signal and slow down until you find the first opportunity to pull over.

152. Where should you pull over, in most instances?

A. Center median
B. Right traffic lane
C. Right shoulder
D. A parking lot off the highway

Correct Answer is C. Right shoulder.

153. How can you help to ensure everyone's safety in a stop?

   A. Pull far enough off to give the officer a place to stand off the roadway
   B. Keep your hands visible
   C. Remain inside your vehicle
   D. All of the above

Correct Answer is D. All of the above.

154. Must you stop if you are in a collision?

   A. Yes
   B. No

Correct Answer is A. Yes.

155. How long do you have to provide a written report to the police or highway patrol if someone is killed or injured in an accident that involves you?

    A. 1 hour
    B. 24 hours
    C. 48 hours
    D. one week

Correct Answer is B. 24 hours.

156. If you hit a parked vehicle or other property, what should you do?

    A. Check for cameras; if you don't see any, drive away
    B. Leave a note with your name and contact information
    C. Call local law enforcement
    D. B & C

Correct Answer is D. B & C.

157. What is the first thing you should do if your vehicle becomes disabled on railroad tracks?

    A. Wait in your car for help to arrive
    B. Call a roadside assistance provider
    C. Exit your vehicle immediately
    D. None of the above

Correct Answer is C. Exit your vehicle immediately.

158. If a train is coming and your car is stalled on the track, where should you run?

    A. Toward the train to signal the driver with your hands
    B. At a 45-degree angle away from the tracks in the direction the train is heading
    C. At a 45-degree angle away from the tracks in the direction the train is coming from
    D. At a 90-degree angle down the road and away from the tracks

Correct Answer is B. At a 45-degree angle away from the tracks in the direction the train is heading.

159. If you stall on railroad tracks and a train is not coming, what do you do?

   A. Call the Emergency Notification System number located on the railroad crossing post or control box at the crossing
   B. Call 911
   C. Both A and B
   D. Neither A nor B — a stalled car is not an emergency

Correct Answer is C. Both A and B.

160. Which of these statements is true about alcohol in a moving motor vehicle?

   A. Drivers must not be drinking while the vehicle is moving
   B. Containers of alcohol in the passenger compartment must be full, sealed, and unopened
   C. Passengers must not be drinking while the vehicle is moving
   D. All of the above

Correct Answer is D. All of the above.

161. Is it OK for a person to ride in the back of a pickup truck?

    A. Yes
    B. No

Correct Answer is B. No.

162. Is it against the law to throw a cigarette from your vehicle?

    A. Yes
    B. No

Correct Answer is A. Yes.

163. Does a funeral procession have the right of way?

   A. Yes
   B. No

Correct Answer is A. Yes.

164. How can you identify a funeral procession?

   A. It is led by a traffic officer
   B. Cars taking part have their lights on
   C. Cars may have windshield markers or flags to identify them
   D. All of the above

Correct Answer is C. Cars may have windshield markers or flags to identify them.

165. Is it legal to alter your license plate?

   A. Yes
   B. No

Correct Answer is B. No.

166. A vehicle is approaching, and you have your high-beams on. How soon must you dim your lights?

   A. Within 100 feet
   B. Within 250 feet
   C. Within 500 feet
   D. Within 1,000 feet

Correct Answer is C. Within 500 feet.

167. You come up behind a vehicle in your lane, and you have your high-beams on. How soon must you dim them?

    A. Within 100 feet
    B. Within 300 feet
    C. Within 500 feet
    D. You don't have to dim your lights

Correct Answer is B. Within 300 feet.

168. Do most states require you to carry proof of insurance?

    A. Yes
    B. No

Correct Answer is A. Yes.

169. What is the leading cause of death for teens in the U.S.?

    A. Cancer
    B. Murder
    C. Car crashes
    D. Suicide

Correct Answer is C. Car crashes.

170. The death rate for teen male drivers and passengers is twice that for females.

    A. True
    B. False

Correct Answer is A. True.

171. Which age group has the highest risk for car crashes?

    A. 16-19
    B. 20-22
    C. 23-25
    D. 26-28

Correct Answer is A. 16-19.

172. Does a regular driver's license apply to a motorcycle?

    A. Yes
    B. No

Correct Answer is B. No.

173. Does a regular driver's license allow a driver to operate a limousine service?

  A. Yes
  B. No

Correct Answer is B. No

174. Does a regular driver's license apply to a commercial truck?

  A. Yes
  B. No

Correct Answer is B. No

175. Before you move your car in reverse, make sure that you ...

   A. Have a clear view out of the back window
   B. Consult your side mirrors
   C. Make sure there are no obstructions behind you
   D. All of the above

Correct Answer is D. All of the above.

176. You are at a red light that turns green. What should you do?

   A. Very quickly accelerate through so that you don't hold up traffic
   B. Wait ten seconds before cautiously moving forward
   C. Politely wave cross-traffic on through
   D. Yield to pedestrians before moving

Correct Answer is D. Yield to pedestrians before moving.

177. Why should you constantly scan the road ahead?

   A. It keeps you awake
   B. It lets you win "I Spy" and the license plate game
   C. You can avoid surprises that might cause a panicked reaction
   D. It makes the trip more interesting

Correct Answer is C. You can avoid surprises that might cause a panicked reaction.

178. What should you do when you're driving in fog in the daytime?

   A. Turn on your headlights on the high-beam setting
   B. Turn on your headlights on the low-beam setting
   C. Turn on your parking lights
   D. Keep all lights off

Correct Answer is B. Turn on your headlights on the low-beam setting.

179. In which lane should you travel if you are driving faster than the other cars on the freeway?

    A. Rightmost regular lane
    B. Leftmost regular lane
    C. Carpool lane
    D. Shoulder

Correct Answer is B. Leftmost regular lane.

180. When are you legally permitted to drive above the speed limit?

    A. When all of the cars around you are driving above the speed limit
    B. When the rest of the traffic are all driving above the speed limit
    C. When you are in an urgent hurry
    D. Never

Correct Answer is D. Never.

181. What turn signal does an arm straight out mean?

    A. Right turn
    B. Left turn
    C. It is not a signal

Correct Answer is B. Left turn.

182. How can you tell if there is a vehicle in your blind spot?

    A. Use your intuition
    B. Ask a passenger
    C. Look over your shoulder
    D. It is impossible to tell

Correct Answer is C. Look over your shoulder.

183. You've had too much to drink. What should you do before driving?

   A. Drink coffee
   B. Eat something
   C. Take a cold shower
   D. Don't drive at all

Correct Answer is D. Don't drive at all.

184. What kind of line marks the right edge of the pavement?

   A. No line
   B. Solid white line
   C. Solid yellow line
   D. A and B

Correct Answer is D. A and B.

185. A fire truck is coming up behind you with its lights and sirens on, but the lane beside you is open for it to pass. Is it OK to continue driving normally instead of pulling over?

    A. Yes
    B. No

Correct Answer is B. No.

186. What should you do when an emergency vehicle is coming up behind you with its lights and sirens on?

    A. Slow down
    B. Pull over to the right
    C. Slow down and pull over to the right
    D. Speed up

Correct Answer is C. Slow down and pull over to the right.

187. **A parallel parking space should be at least how many feet longer than your vehicle?**

   A. 1
   B. 2
   C. 3
   D. 4

Correct Answer is C. 3.

188. **What is the first thing you should do when you arrive at a parallel parking spot where you intend to park?**

   A. Pull in
   B. Back in
   C. Beep
   D. Activate your turn signal

Correct Answer is D. Activate your turn signal.

189. What color is used to indicate handicapped parking?

    A. White
    B. Yellow
    C. Green
    D. Blue

Correct Answer is D. Blue.

190. Which of the following are examples of handicapped placard abuse?

    A. Using a placard that belongs to a friend or family member
    B. Loaning your placard to a friend or family member
    C. Using a placard for a household member who is not in the vehicle with you
    D. All of the above

Correct Answer is D. All of the above.

191. Is it OK to use the handicapped placard of a deceased family member?

    A. Sure
    B. Of course not

Correct Answer is B. Of course not.

192. Is it legal to park in an unmarked crosswalk?

    A. Yes
    B. No

Correct Answer is B. No.

193. How many feet away from a sidewalk ramp or a wheelchair access point must you park?

    A. 1
    B. 3
    C. 5
    D. 10

Correct Answer is B. 3.

194. Why is a space next to a disabled parking space sometimes marked with a crosshatched/diagonal pattern?

    A. To show that it is OK for non-disabled people to park there
    B. To allow loading and unloading space for the disabled person, including portable ramp usage
    C. To provide a spot for people who are hurt but don't have a placard
    D. Nobody knows for sure

Correct Answer is B. To allow loading and unloading space for the disabled person, including portable ramp usage.

195. How many feet are you required to maintain when parking by a fire hydrant or fire station driveway?

    A. 5
    B. 10
    C. 15
    D. 20

Correct Answer is C. 15.

196. Is it OK to park in a tunnel or on a bridge?

    A. Yes, if permitted by signs
    B. Yes, any time
    C. No, never
    D. Yes, if it is a very wide tunnel or bridge

Correct Answer is A. Yes, if permitted by signs.

197. When sharing a lane with a bicycle, how many feet of clearance should you give?

   A. 5 Feet
   B. 3 Feet
   C. 10 Feet
   D. None

Correct Answer is B. 3 Feet.

198. Is it OK to parallel park on the opposite side of the street from the direction in which you are traveling when it is not a one-way street?

   A. No
   B. Yes

Correct Answer is A. No.

199. Is it legal to park on a freeway?

    A. No, never
    B. Yes, in an emergency
    C. Yes, when you are being pulled over by law enforcement
    D. B & C

Correct Answer is D. B & C.

200. When is it legal to turn right on red?

    A. It is never legal
    B. It is always legal
    C. When there is no sign indicating that a right turn on red is illegal
    D. None of the above

Correct Answer is C. When there is no sign indicating that a right turn on red is illegal.

201. When four cars are stopped at a four-way intersection, which one should go first?

- A. The first vehicle to have arrived
- B. The vehicle to your right
- C. The biggest or most powerful vehicle
- D. None of the above

Correct Answer is A. The first vehicle to have arrived.

202. When driving what should you do when it rains?

- A. Turn on your headlights
- B. Turn on your windshield wipers
- C. Turn on your headlights and your windshield wipers
- D. Pull off the road and wait for the rain to stop

Correct Answer is C. Turn on your headlights and your windshield wipers.

203. Where might you find a slick spot on the road?

   A. In shady areas
   B. On overpasses or bridges
   C. In low areas
   D. All of the above

Correct Answer is D. All of the above.

204. There is oncoming traffic in your lane, but you're right where you're supposed to be. What do you do?

   A. Pull off to the right shoulder
   B. Flash your lights
   C. Beep your horn
   D. All of the above

Correct Answer is D. All of the above.

205. What color are the lane markings that separate multiple lanes of traffic moving in the same direction?

A. White
B. Yellow
C. Red
D. Blue

Correct Answer is A. White.

206. What color are the lane markings that separate lanes of traffic moving in opposite directions?

A. White
B. Yellow
C. Red
D. Blue

Correct Answer is B. Yellow.

207. When you are driving, you should look this far ahead:

A. 3 seconds
B. 5 seconds
C. 10 seconds
D. 20 seconds

Correct Answer is C. 10 seconds.

208. You see a flashing yellow light. What does it mean?

A. Stop and then move forward slowly
B. Proceed slowly and cautiously
C. Lane ends
D. None of the above

Correct Answer is B. Proceed slowly and cautiously.

209. You are in an intersection when you hear a siren from an emergency vehicle. What should you do?

   A. Stop right where you are until the emergency vehicle passes
   B. Back up and pull to the right to stop your car
   C. Proceed through the intersection and then pull to the right side to stop your car
   D. None of the above

Correct Answer is C. Proceed through the intersection and then pull to the right side to stop your car.

210. You are at a railroad crossing marked by a sign but with no signal. What should you do?

   A. Drive across as quickly as you can
   B. Approach slowly and look carefully both ways
   C. Stop, roll down your window, and listen
   D. None of the above

Correct Answer is B. Approach slowly and look carefully both ways.

211. You are parking on a hill facing downward. Where do you point your tires?

    A. Toward the curb
    B. Away from the curb
    C. Straight
    D. None of the above

Correct Answer is A. Toward the curb.

212. What dangerous practice is also illegal to perform while driving?

    A. Driving one-handed
    B. Wearing headphones over your ears
    C. Eating
    D. Reading a map

Correct Answer is B. Wearing headphones over your ears.

213. Does talking on a cell phone increase your chance of being in an accident?

- A. Yes, by a factor of four
- B. Yes, but just slightly
- C. No
- D. No one knows for sure

Correct Answer is A. Yes, by a factor of four.

214. What color curb means you can stop to pick up or drop off passengers or mail?

- A. White
- B. Green
- C. Yellow
- D. Red

Correct Answer is A. White.

215. What color curb means you can park for a limited time, usually explained in a sign?

    A. White
    B. Green
    C. Yellow
    D. Red

Correct Answer is B. Green.

216. What color curb means you cannot stop, stand, or park at all?

    A. White
    B. Green
    C. Yellow
    D. Red

Correct Answer is D. Red.

217. What color curb means you can stop to load or unload passengers or freight for a stated amount of time?

    A. White
    B. Green
    C. Yellow
    D. Red

Correct Answer is C. Yellow.

218. What factors influence how our bodies absorb alcohol?

    A. Time between each drink
    B. Weight of drinker
    C. Amount of food in the stomach
    D. All of the above

Correct Answer is D. All of the above.

219. Is it ever legal to make a left turn on red?

   A. No
   B. Yes, when the cross street is completely empty
   C. Yes, when the red light is taking too long
   D. Yes, when moving from left lane of one one-way street to the left lane of another one-way street

Correct Answer is D. Yes, when moving from left lane of one one-way street to the left lane of another one-way street.

220. You're on a four-lane road and approaching a school bus with its yellow lights flashing. What should you do?

   A. Stop until the bus moves on after letting off a student
   B. Slow down but proceed cautiously since the red lights aren't on
   C. Speed up to beat the stopping signal
   D. Move to the far-right lane and proceed as normal

Correct Answer is B. Slow down but proceed cautiously since the red lights aren't on.

221. If you are on the other side of a four-lane road and you approach a bus with its red flashing lights displayed, what should you do?

    A. Slow down and move cautiously past
    B. Stop
    C. Move to the far-right lane and proceed as normal
    D. Speed up

Correct Answer is B. Stop.

222. Children between the ages of 4 and 8 are required to be in a booster seat while in a moving vehicle unless the child is _____.

    A. 4'5" or taller
    B. 4'9" or taller
    C. 5' or taller
    D. In sixth grade or above

Correct Answer is B. 4'9" or taller.

223. When are booster seats not required for children meeting age and height requirements for one?

   A. In public safety vehicles
   B. In taxi cabs
   C. In vehicles not required by law to have safety belts when manufactured
   D. All of the above

Correct Answer is D. All of the above.

224. What does the law say about carrying cargo in a passenger vehicle?

   A. Cargo shall never be carried in a passenger vehicle
   B. Cargo may be carried only in the trunk of a passenger vehicle
   C. Cargo may not obstruct the driver's vision
   D. There are not laws about cargo in a passenger vehicle

Correct Answer is C. Cargo may not obstruct the driver's vision.

225. What blood-alcohol concentration level minimally classifies a driver as impaired?

    A. .05%
    B. .08%
    C. .1%
    D. 1%

Correct Answer is B. .08%.

226. True or false: You can lose driving privileges if you use a fake ID to buy alcohol.

    A. True
    B. False

Correct Answer is A. True.

227. You are approaching a sign that depicts a truck heading downward on the slope of a triangle. What does this mean?

    A. Truck mechanic services available
    B. Downgrade ahead
    C. Trucks must exit
    D. Tracks backing ahead

Correct Answer is B. Downgrade ahead.

228. What is the message being conveyed by a sign with a rising arrow pointing at a 90-degree angle to the right or left?

    A. Intersection ahead
    B. Town or city ahead
    C. Sharp turn to the right or left ahead
    D. Numerous curves ahead

Correct Answer is C. Sharp turn to the right or left ahead.

229. What if a sign shows a rising arrow with a 90-degree angle to the right, then another 90-degree angle to the left, so that the arrow is pointing straight up?

   A. Sharp turn to the left and then to the right
   B. Sharp turn to the right and then to the left
   C. Multiple sharp turns ahead
   D. Bumpy road ahead

Correct Answer is B. Sharp turn to the right and then to the left.

230. What does a black cross on a yellow sign mean?

   A. Church ahead
   B. Funeral home ahead
   C. Cemetery ahead
   D. Crossroads/intersection ahead

Correct Answer is D. Crossroads/intersection ahead.

231. A yellow sign depicts a black arrow with a line extending out to the right from its center. What does this mean?

    A. A road comes from the right to form a T-intersection with the road you are on
    B. A road comes from the left to form a T-intersection with the road you are on
    C. A town is located to your right
    D. You are crossing the city or county line

Correct Answer is A. A road comes from the right to form a T-intersection with the road you are on.

232. You approach a yellow sign with the words "ONE-LANE BRIDGE" on it. What should you do?

    A. Be aware of a local attraction
    B. Proceed with caution, noting that the vehicle closest to the bridge has the right of way
    C. Proceed quickly, regardless of oncoming traffic, to clear the bridge for the next vehicle that needs it
    D. Find another route

Correct Answer is B. Proceed with caution, noting that the vehicle closest to the bridge has the right of way.

233. A yellow sign depicts what looks like a capital letter Y. What does this indicate?

   A. Life is meaningless
   B. The road branches to the right and left ahead
   C. Stay to the right
   D. YMCA ahead

Correct Answer is B. The road branches to the right and left ahead.

234. A yellow sign depicts black measurements (example: 12'-6") with arrows pointing above and below. What is it trying to tell you?

   A. Your car must be this tall to enter
   B. Clearance is limited by a bridge, tunnel, overhead crosswalk, etc.
   C. Flooding can reach 12 feet, 6 inches in this location
   D. The next town is this far away

Correct Answer is B. Clearance is limited by a bridge, tunnel, overhead crosswalk, etc.

235. A yellow sign depicts two black arrows side by side; one is pointing up, and the other is pointing down. What does this indicate?

A. You can go either way to get to your destination
B. Hills go up and down ahead
C. Traffic is moving in both directions
D. Detour ahead will reroute you back to the road you are on

Correct Answer is C. Traffic is moving in both directions.

236. A yellow sign shows the outline of the rear of a black car with what looks like skid marks behind it. What does this signify?

A. The road ahead is slippery when wet
B. There is deep mud on the road ahead
C. Snow is on the road ahead
D. Do no donuts

Correct Answer is A. The road ahead is slippery when wet.

237. A yellow sign depicts a leaping deer. What does it mean?

   A. No hunting
   B. Deer crossing
   C. Animal preserve
   D. Scenic overlook

Correct Answer is B. Deer crossing.

238. A yellow sign depicts a black bicycle. What does it mean?

   A. Share the road with bicycles
   B. Bicycle crossing
   C. Trail access ahead
   D. You should be biking for the environment

Correct Answer is B. Bicycle crossing.

239. Your tire blows, and your vehicle is suddenly difficult to control. What should you do?

    A. Maintain firm control of steering wheel while releasing pressure on the gas pedal
    B. Slam on the brakes
    C. Speed up and pull off the road quickly
    D. Turn on your hazard lights and drive to the next exit

Correct Answer is A. Maintain firm control of steering wheel while releasing pressure on the gas pedal.

240. An orange sign depicts a human form with a square coming out from the left hand and the right hand raised. What does this mean?

    A. Charity collecting donations ahead
    B. Flagger ahead
    C. Welcome to our city
    D. Detour ahead

Correct Answer is B. Flagger ahead.

241. An orange sign says "ROAD WORK AHEAD." What could this mean?

   A. Road work is currently happening on the road ahead
   B. Road work will be coming within the next year
   C. Help is wanted by the road department
   D. Road work has recently been completed on the road ahead

Correct Answer is A. Road work is currently happening on the road ahead.

242. What color combination is not used to denote guide signs?

   A. Blue and white
   B. Green and white
   C. Red and blue
   D. Brown and white

Correct Answer is C. Red and blue.

243. To show travelers how to find a hospital, a blue sign is erected with what symbol?

A. A picture of a hospital
B. A picture of a hospital bed
C. The letter H
D. A stethoscope

Correct Answer is C. The letter H.

244. You see a white sign depicting an arrow that rises, curves back on itself, and then points straight down, and there is a red prohibition symbol across it. What does this mean?

A. Road blocked ahead
B. No curves ahead
C. U-turns are not permitted
D. Be observant

Correct Answer is C. U-turns are not permitted.

245. You see a white sign depicting a black bicycle with a red prohibition symbol across it. What does this mean?

    A. Bikes are not permitted on this road
    B. Cars are not permitted on this road
    C. Motorcycles are not permitted on this road
    D. Cars do not need to yield to bicycles

Correct Answer is A. Bikes are not permitted on this road.

246. The road you are on has a right lane with northbound traffic, a left lane with southbound traffic, and a middle lane marked with two white arrows, one pointing left and one pointing right with no separation between them. What do the arrows mean?

    A. Turn lane; cars may turn left but not right
    B. Turn lane; cars may turn right but not left
    C. Turn lane; cars may turn in either direction
    D. This lane is not for traffic

Correct Answer is C. Turn lane; cars may turn in either direction.

247. You've hit a deer and caused its death. Can you take it home to eat it?

    A. No
    B. Yes — no other steps required
    C. Yes, if you report it to a game protector or law enforcement within 24 hours
    D. Yes, if you field-dress it on the spot

Correct Answer is C. Yes, if you report it to a game protector or law enforcement within 24 hours.

248. Your car has gone into a skid. How do you steer out of it?

    A. Turn in the direction of the skid
    B. Turn away from the skid
    C. Hold the steering wheel steady
    D. Slam on the brakes and steer when you have stopped

Correct Answer is A. Turn in the direction of the skid.

249. What does it mean to be a defensive driver?

A. The best defense is a good offense; be aggressive
B. Be mindful of other drivers and be alert for their possible mistakes
C. Notify other drivers with your horn when they are wrong
D. Carry a weapon in your car

Correct Answer is B. Be mindful of other drivers and be alert for their possible mistakes.

250. When is it OK to double-park?

A. When it's an emergency
B. When you plan to be back to your car very quickly
C. When there is sufficient room for other cars to get by
D. Never

Correct Answer is D. Never.

251. You want to turn left at an intersection, but traffic in the oncoming lane is heavy. What should you do?

    A. Wait behind the retaining line for the traffic to clear
    B. Enter the intersection and wait for the traffic to clear
    C. Turn and force the oncoming traffic to stop
    D. None of the above

Correct Answer is B. Enter the intersection and wait for the traffic to clear.

252. When may you cross a solid yellow line?

    A. To turn into a driveway on the left side of the road
    B. To pass a car
    C. To see around a big truck
    D. You can never do this

Correct Answer is A. To turn into a driveway on the left side of the road.

253. When is it OK to park next to a fire hydrant?

   A. When you are just going to be a short time away from your car
   B. When nearby buildings are not on fire
   C. When you are willing to move your vehicle in case of emergency
   D. When you are the driver of the fire truck responding to an emergency

Correct Answer is D. When you are the driver of the fire truck responding to an emergency.

254. What do orange road signs indicate?

   A. Hazard ahead
   B. Construction ahead
   C. Tollbooth ahead
   D. School zone

Correct Answer is B. Construction ahead.

255. You plan to turn onto a roadway just after an intersection. When should you signal?

    A. Before you cross the intersection
    B. After you cross the intersection
    C. In the middle of the intersection
    D. Not at all

Correct Answer is B. After you cross the intersection.

256. When might you choose to use hand signals while driving?

    A. If your car's signaling device is not functioning
    B. If you are driving into bright sun
    C. Never
    D. A & B

Correct Answer is D. A & B.

257. How many feet ahead of your turn should you signal?

   A. 25
   B. 50
   C. 100
   D. 200

Correct Answer is C. 100.

258. What should you do before changing lanes?

   A. Check mirrors
   B. Check blind spot
   C. Use signal
   D. All of the above

Correct Answer is D. All of the above.

259. On a freeway, you should signal ___ seconds before you change lanes.

   A. 3
   B. 5
   C. 10
   D. 12

Correct Answer is B. 5.

260. If you do not see other vehicles, you do not need to signal.

   A. True
   B. False

Correct Answer is B. False.

261. It is best to drive with two hands on the wheel, if you have them.

   A. True
   B. False

Correct Answer is A. True.

262. Is it OK to use a horn to encourage a slow driver or bicyclist to speed up or get out of the way?

   A. Yes
   B. No

Correct Answer is B. No.

263. Why should you not honk at other drivers to criticize their driving?

A. You could startle them
B. You could elicit an angry reaction or retaliation
C. You may miss an obstruction or other situation that caused their seemingly erratic driving
D. All of the above

Correct Answer is D. All of the above.

264. When you need to use your windshield wipers, you are required to use your headlights.

A. True
B. False

Correct Answer is A. True.

265. When should you use your headlights?

   A. In rain or snow
   B. In dust, smoke, or fog
   C. When it's dark outside
   D. All of the above

Correct Answer is D. All of the above.

266. How many minutes after sunset and before sunrise should you use your headlights?

   A. 10
   B. 20
   C. 30
   D. 60

Correct Answer is C. 30.

267. When should you use your emergency flashers?

    A. If you see a collision ahead and wish to warn other drivers
    B. If your vehicle breaks down
    C. If conditions force you to drive slowly
    D. All of the above

Correct Answer is D. All of the above.

268. You experience car trouble while driving on the freeway. What should you do?

    A. Pull off the road and away from traffic
    B. Stop where you can be seen from behind
    C. Lift hood to signal the need for help
    D. All of the above

Correct Answer is D. All of the above.

269. You are driving on a two-lane road. There is a bicyclist operating in your lane in front of you and an oncoming vehicle in the other lane. What is the best driving practice here?

    A. Go quickly around the bicyclist before the approach car can reach you
    B. Slow or stop to let the approaching vehicle pass and then go around the bicyclist
    C. Proceed as normal, allowing everyone to take care of their own safety needs
    D. Beep at the bicyclist, who can then move to the sidewalk

Correct Answer is B. Slow or stop to let the approaching vehicle pass and then go around the bicyclist.

270. You should take extra care around children. Why?

    A. They may run into the street without warning
    B. They may be unstable or erratic in their movement patterns
    C. They don't fully understand the dangers of traffic
    D. All of the above

Correct Answer is D. All of the above.

271. You're trying to move onto a busy freeway. Who has the right of way?

    A. You
    B. Freeway traffic
    C. Whoever is fastest
    D. Whoever is biggest

Correct Answer is B. Freeway traffic.

272. In general, should you stop before merging onto a freeway?

    A. Yes
    B. No

Correct Answer is B. No.

273. Why is it more dangerous to drive at night?

   A. You're more likely to be fatigued
   B. The distance you can see is reduced
   C. Animal activity may increase
   D. All of the above

Correct Answer is D. All of the above.

274. This word refers to following the car in front of you too closely:

   A. Tailwagging
   B. Tailgating
   C. Reargating
   D. Rearwagging

Correct Answer is B. Tailgating.

275. This term for making a series of unnecessary lane changes comes from the world of crafts:

   A. Knitting
   B. Purling
   C. Weaving
   D. Macrame

Correct Answer is C. Weaving.

276. Our behaviors can contribute to congestion. Some of these include the following:

   A. Following too closely
   B. Making unnecessary lane changes
   C. Not paying attention
   D. All of the above

Correct Answer is D. All of the above.

277. What should you do to maintain safety before entering a curve?

   A. Slow down
   B. Speed up
   C. Beep your horn
   D. Flash your lights

Correct Answer is A. Slow down.

278. When there is water on the road and you are traveling at a speed of 50 mph or more, you may lose contact with the road. What is this called?

   A. Skiing
   B. Parasailing
   C. Hydroplaning
   D. Tobogganing

Correct Answer is C. Hydroplaning.

279. How much slower should you travel on a wet road?

    A. No slower — just be more watchful
    B. 5-10 mph slower
    C. 10-15 mph slower
    D. Slightly faster to control the slide

Correct Answer is B. 5-10 mph slower.

280. How should you drive on packed snow?

    A. Exactly the same as in typical conditions
    B. At half your normal speed
    C. With side-to-side motions to keep traction
    D. Slightly faster than usual

Correct Answer is B. At half your normal speed.

281. What are some precautions to take when driving into sun glare?

    A. Keep inside and outside of your windshield clean
    B. Wear polarized sunglasses
    C. Be confident and drive as normal on familiar roads
    D. A & B

Correct Answer is D. A & B.

282. An approaching car has its bright headlights on, making it hard for you to see. What is the best strategy for staying in your lane?

    A. Keep your eye on the yellow center line
    B. Keep your eye on the white line at the right side of the road
    C. Gauge your lane placement off the location of the oncoming car
    D. None of the above

Correct Answer is B. Keep your eye on the white line at the right side of the road.

283. What are some signs that your tires may be in need of replacement?

    A. Tears in the side of the tire
    B. Depleted treads
    C. Bulges in the side of the tire
    D. All of the above

Correct Answer is D. All of the above.

284. How can you check your tire health with a penny?

    A. You can flip it — heads, replace the tire; tails, you're fine
    B. You can place it with Lincoln's head pointing downward into a tread; if you can see any part of his head, you need new tires
    C. Rub the penny beside your tire; if it turns black, replace your tires
    D. Run over the penny with the tire; if it flattens, replace your tires

Correct Answer is B. You can place it with Lincoln's head pointing downward into a tread; if you can see any part of his head, you need new tires.

285. Is it true that the risk of driver fatality increases with each passenger added to a vehicle driven by a 16- or 17-year-old driver?

A. Yes
B. No

Correct Answer is A. Yes.

286. Throughout the United States, people drive on the _____ side of the road.

A. Left
B. Right
C. Center
D. Least congested

Correct Answer is B. Right.

287. In the U.K. and most former British colonies, people drive on the _____ side of the road.

   A. Left
   B. Right
   C. Center
   D. Least congested

Correct Answer is A. Left.

288. What is the typical speed limit for an alley within a city?

   A. 5 mph
   B. 15 mph
   C. 20 mph
   D. There is no typical speed limit

Correct Answer is B. 15 mph.

289. What is the typical speed limit for a school zone while children are present?

    A. 5 mph
    B. 15 mph
    C. 20 mph
    D. There is no typical speed limit

Correct Answer is C. 20 mph.

290. What is the typical speed limit for a regular road (not a state route or a highway) within a city?

    A. 15 mph
    B. 25 mph
    C. 40 mph
    D. There is no typical speed limit

Correct Answer is B. 25 mph.

291. What is the typical speed for a state route or through highway (except for a controlled-access highway) within a city?

    A. 25 mph
    B. 35 mph
    C. 45 mph
    D. There is no typical speed limit

Correct Answer is B. 35 mph.

292. What is the typical speed for state routes within municipal corporations outside urban districts, unless a lower speed is established visibly on a sign?

    A. 25 mph
    B. 35 mph
    C. 50 mph
    D. There is no typical speed limit

Correct Answer is C. 50 mph.

293. When is a minimum speed limit in effect?

A. When posted
B. When significantly low speeds are a danger to other drivers
C. A & B
D. There is no such thing as a minimum speed

Correct Answer is C. A & B.

294. When is it OK to race on a public road?

A. It is never legal to race on a public road
B. When the public road is empty
C. When the racers have permission from property owners
D. Always

Correct Answer is A. It is never legal to race on a public road.

295. Suppose you just organized a race on a public road but did not participate. Can you be charged with a legal infraction?

    A. No
    B. Yes, but only if money was exchanged
    C. Yes, but only if the race is a regular event
    D. Yes

Correct Answer is D. Yes.

296. Which of these warning devices might you encounter before a railroad crossing?

    A. Pavement markings consisting of an "X" and an "RR"
    B. Railroad cross buck signs
    C. Gates
    D. All of the above

Correct Answer is D. All of the above.

297. What must a school bus do before a railroad crossing?

    A. Let out all passengers to walk across
    B. Come to a complete stop
    C. Turn around and find another route
    D. None of the above

Correct Answer is B. Come to a complete stop.

298. Is it legal to drive around a lowered railroad gate?

    A. Yes, if no train is in sight
    B. Yes, if train is 500 yards away
    C. Yes
    D. No

Correct Answer is D. No.

299. Many states have mandatory seat belt laws. Which statement is true?

A. A seat belt ticket is a moving violation; an infraction will go on your driving record
B. A seat belt ticket is not a moving violation; no infraction will go on your driving record
C. A seat belt ticket carries no penalty at all
D. There is no such thing as a seat belt violation

Correct Answer is A. A seat belt ticket is a moving violation; an infraction will go on your driving record.

300. Who must be properly restrained in an approved child safety seat?

A. Children under the age of 4
B. Children who weigh less than 40 pounds
C. Children who are either or both under the age of 4 and weigh less than 40 pounds
D. No one is required to be restrained in a child safety seat if seat belts are present

Correct Answer is C. Children who are either or both under the age of 4 and weigh less than 40 pounds.

301. Teenage drivers are most likely to get into a car crash when:

A. They are driving with adult passengers in the car
B. They are driving without any passengers in the car
C. They are driving with no teenage passengers in the car
D. They are driving with friends in the car

Correct Answer is D. They are driving with friends in the car.